AF266187

The unconstructible machine

The unconstructible machine

the unconstructible machine

& other essays · martin firrell

martin firrell company
PUBLIC CONVERSATIONS OF SOCIAL VALUE

First published in 2017 by Martin Firrell Company Ltd,
10 Queen Street Place, London EC4R 1AG, United Kingdom.

ISBN 978-0-9931786-8-9

© Copyright Martin Firrell 2017

Martin Firrell has asserted his right under the Copyright, Designs and Patents Act 1988 to be identified as the author of this work.

All rights reserved. No part of this publication may be reproduced, stored in or introduced into a retrieval system, or transmitted, in any form, or by any means (electronic, mechanical, photocopying, recording or otherwise) without the prior written consent of the publisher.

This book is sold subject to the condition that it shall not, by way of trade or otherwise, be lent, re-sold, hired out, or otherwise circulated without the publisher's prior consent in any form of binding or cover other than that in which it is published and without a similar condition including this condition being imposed on the subsequent purchaser.

CONTENTS

CONTENTS

PREFACE

The texts in this short volume were written more than 20 years ago between 1994 and 1997. I was interested at that time in exploring impossibility, mystery, unsolvable problems and improbable outcomes.

I was young – in all likelihood younger than my years – and trying to make sense of the tangle of the world.

I was also trying to shape an approach to language which would serve me in my work to come.

I have divided the texts, for the purposes of this publication, into Theoretical Writing and Experimental Writing – the exploration of theory informs the experimental texts that follow.

These texts are juvenilia, without a doubt. But I think they are worth preserving and sharing because in the naïveté of my view all those years ago, something of interest and some kind of truth was caught.

My subsequent work as a public artist rests in many ways on the tentative experimentalism that follows.

Martin Firrell, Soho, London 2017.

THEORETICAL WRITING

THE LAST WILD TEA ORCHID

*I am like someone blindfolded trying to remember objects on
a tray.*

I do not know what I am. I do not know what I will become.

I have no idea how to live.

*I try to know myself. But I am only the remembrance
of myself –*

*The more I come to know what I am, the more I alter what
I will become.*

*Everything I discover about myself is altered by the action of
discovery – as in the case of the last wild tea orchid plucked
from the wild.*

THE ONE WORD NOVEL

Seen from a very great distance, the surf does not break. Never seen before, there would be no sensation of the waves sitting up. Distance diminishes the surf to a scattering of points which open, thicken, famine, die away.

Collapse and telescope the distance-reduced sea, the running tide, the estuary, the beach, the terns, nesting grounds, shingle, walking, swimming, drying stretched out over the sharp points of flint.

He must have known the way to walk the flats, between the samphire and the twisted lines of the creeks, across the estuary to the point. Rucksack swaying from one brown shoulder. Alive. Unhurrying. Passing the last of the dunes before the sea. Mud caked and drying already against his legs.

A tempered language to give the whole of the intention with the least possible distortion.

One. Brown. Shoulder. Unweighted. The sun still hot, the sea, the blown-paper gulls.

Language shaped to contain what it cannot describe. Making a habitat for, rather than a record of, an intention. The accommodating word.

Ribs. Standing out. Like piano keys.

The original intention has its existence, its reason to be, inside the word rather than words having their existence, their reason to be, inside the original intention.

Language unbroken but reduced to the smallest irreducible component. Like the irreducible particle at the heart of an atom. The extraordinary holding capacity of the word. The struck word echoes. The whole of the intention conveyed with completeness because the intention has all of its existence inside a word, rather than words giving a composite, spider's eye representation of the intention.

The heat, the swaying rucksack, the network of muddy creeks effortlessly conquered (even though the sign said it was dangerous to cross at all states of the tide), the reduced, airless sea, the clear heat of midday, the pain of self consciousness, all held in the eye of the one, reliable and unbreakable word: BURN.

ON AESTHETICS

What is there more beautiful than justice?

THE UNCONSTRUCTIBLE MACHINE

The unconstructible machine is the triumph of absolute brevity over form. It is freed entirely of physical flaw and inaccuracy because it never has, nor ever will exist in the material world.

The unconstructible machine doesn't exist because it cannot exist. It is too delicate, too many-pivoted, too elaborate and beautiful to exist. It would buckle and collapse under its own weight like a blue whale out of water.

The machine is known to us as a thing incapable of existence and in this sense, even though it remains unrealised, it exists: rare, fragile, otherworldly, improbably conceived and unfathomably mechanised.

The unconstructible machine exists without realisation, as expression without form, as uncastable sculpture.

This expression without realisation is the thing most perfectly, most fluidly and flexibly created.

We have few opportunities to see for seeing's sake because of the demands made on us by the daily action of living.

But the machine is not living. It is not, does not, exists not. It has no utility whatsoever.

Absolutely unfitted for everyday existence, the unconstructible machine throws our attention elsewhere.

We are prompted to enquire in a direction we would never normally consider because we are never, in the normal course of our daily lives, confronted by a nonentity whose purpose is absolutely nothing and whose absolute unfitness for everything is its purpose.

The unconstructible machine has no inner or outer, no interior or underneath, it hides nothing, encloses nothing, encompasses everything: explanation, composition in its widest sense, critical mind, the true critical mind that attempts to understand not by observation alone but with full knowledge of the complexities (and impossibility) of construction.

I am the machine. I am elaborate and beautiful. We all are the machine. Clean, brilliant, airless, rigorous, absolute.

Brilliant mystery – its moment enquiry – spun on the fulcrum paradox. It is this paradox at the heart of the mechanism, it is this paradox that alters the nature of our understanding.

The familiar becomes unfamiliar, the ordinary, extraordinary, the mundane beautiful. 'All the world is Paris & this moment of absolute awareness & receptivity to the beauty in everything is enlightenment.' Say no more, do no more, simply go back to the machine.

This moment is in some way safeguarded, freed of the threat of pollution. It is not public but private. What is a life but the realisation of this moment? There is a requirement to do nothing, only to be.

I sit in this room and Am. I contemplate the unbuildable, the inexpressible, the unresolvable and somehow it is built, expressed, resolved. The machine turns and its sound is the sound of the percussion of being. I see and it is more than seeing. I hear and it is more than hearing.

The machine is liberty or the earthly concept of love or humanity's image of itself. It does not matter.

There lies the critical paradox that makes of absolutely nothing a perfectable masterwork.

This absence is my masterpiece ('It is inadmissible that a man should leave any trace of his passage on earth.'), this omission my genius ('It's hard being a genius. You have to sit around so much doing nothing'). In not existing the machine is complete. It is done because it is not done.

ON POTENTIAL

Consciousness exists in an endless and unseizable state of motion. This motion is driven by the constant upwelling of consciousness's awareness that it is itself aware.

Potential is the straw at which we clutch. The free, the wide, the unbounded entity as super-mirror to the continual and inescapable 'motion of the mind'.

The motion of the mind supersedes and makes obsolete any idea that has become an actuality. An idea suggests limitless promise. Execution of that idea represents only limit.

To reflect the nature of consciousness a different form is needed. Something with sustained potential, freed of inflexible form, uncastable – a super-articulated sculpture, an expression in a continual state of development driven, like consciousness, by the accumulation of the memory of itself.

[Illustration of cardboard sculpture, now lost, titled under the influence of Marinetti's Futurism: Toward the realisation of the potential for the existence of form partially modified by the accumulation of the memory of itself.]

How can any form attain synchronicity with the unending motion of the mind? By being itself also in an unending state of motion, unendingly pertinent, unanticipated, self-renewing.

If the thing spirit resides anywhere, it resides — running like oil or sugar syrup — in the unseizable region of continual transition, progression, development and growth.

Potential can be sustained only by allusion and suggestion.

What form can ever express understanding continually modified by the accumulation of the understanding of itself?

Only something that may never be communicable in its entirety to another living soul.

This apparent tentativeness is genius.

CATEGORY ESSAY

'The roof of my little cat's mouth is rippled like the sea floor' is remarkable because of the words that attach themselves to the sight of my cat's unstifled yawn.

Remarkable: to attempt to look to what stands beyond all this, to what can be reduced from these details.

Then there are the little domestic details and sudden impressions and a whole world filled with light. The way 'who I am' relates to those domestic details and darting, fish-quick impressions.

My cat yawns again and the roof of his mouth is rippled like the sea floor. Rippled like slipped-down socks.

A leaf tunnel bows over us as we cycle, with the sun high up behind the canopy of the trees and all the veins clear to see in every leaf.

A variety of acer is a forest of hands.

Small candied fruits in an exhibition of Spanish still life, pale figs, sugared to a ghostly, lucid cream. Pellucid fruits (is that even possible?) and slaughtered lambs. And hung songbirds: larks, goldfinches.

Is it possible adequately to convey the facts and details of a life? Then systematically to reduce those elements to their essential content. Then allow the language that labels these details to consume itself. The little incidents and customs that make up a life are consumed, lost. Then what will remain?

And when we came home from our cycle we worked in the garden hoeing the gravel, weeding, raking until it looked so lovely with the sunshine on it: white orris irises, daisies, buttercups, euphorbias and the little box edge. The garden table with a little green vase filled with pinks and lily-of-the-valley, the table laid with the 30s Woods Ivory Ware painted with daffodils. On the chest, a basket of oranges and lemons with the sun on it. Outside, the sun lowering behind the cow parsley, everything light-filled, three-dimensional.

We cycled downhill, through a tunnel of trees and out into the sunlight. Dark-light. Motion of the wind – a sense of airiness and freedom. But of course none of this captures it.

'A basket of oranges with the sun on it.' Doesn't capture it.

The day doesn't live again.

Is a cat a fully given, fully expressed thing to itself. Unthinking. But fully given over to the role and obligation of being a cat? A perfect expression of what it is to be a cat. The impossibility of chipping away at the surface. Can a cat be a fully given thing from behind the surface idea of cat? And can what's true for a cat be true for a man?

The constant digging behind.

The grass is dry. Brown straw over grey dust.

And a thing must be thrown to one side, set at an angle, cast off a little. So that one thing becomes another.

Overlooking the 'View to Infinity' like the balcony in the garden at Ravello. But it is much graver than that.

Suppose a meticulous, laborious description of real life. It would be the description of anything describable. The dullness and weight of it would make the description destroy itself. The whole of real life would weigh in on itself. What was caused to go, to be put beyond reach because of the weight and tedium would leave behind it what could not be weighted down.

Where equality fails, feeling must eventually fail, too.

Language does not connect us but divides us. But equally what is left unsaid may stand between us. Some simple twist —something that throws our expectations off kilter. We are strangely rebuked. Things are not quite as they seem or should be. Real life is far more important to us than reported life. But it remains unknown to us if it is not reported. Perhaps real life is unknowable. And the greatest mistake of all is to read reported life as if it were the real thing. The act of reporting enlarges, makes overly bright the life reported. The question becomes, how to catch real life without *blowing it up a mile high? 'A true story' should be dull, uneventful, uneven, without pace or shape. A hazy cloud that the light of reporting cannot burn off. Keeping to scale. Preventing the sudden inflation of drama. Oppressive, and dead-weighted. Avoiding happy coincidences, and fate. This is real life.*

Real life is long, slow, close to the ground. No sweeping changes of circumstance or instantaneous changes of scene. Weight. Force of detail. Weighing in behind real life. Reported life is too distant, too removed. Say now. Say real life. Now do a thing. Now With weight. With mass, with momentum. Gathering. Weight. Reflection. A backward glance. One backward glance. And go. Go forward with mass, weight, momentum. Streaming real life. Given Unaccountable. Is it done? Can someone do that? It is done. Hold on. Is this wise? Show me wisdom. Now. Dissonant, forcing. Forced. Forceful. Given. Take this. Have this. This is real life. This is not reported but swift, knowing, heavy with detail, repetition, boredom, dullness, immateriality, exhaustion, vigour, boredom, breathlessness, real life. Direct, here, now, lost in report, wild, vital in its weight, its unforgiveableness, its realness. The intention that cannot find form in words.

The formality of the word for its own sake.

Reducing language to its formal properties, light, open, precise, austere, rigorous, analytical, dissipated.

Take the passion from language and what is left?

What if the seeker, is at the same time the dark region through which it must go seeking?

The word beyond the speaker.

LAGOON CITY

Intention is the prize. Closest to the source, the origin, the first thinking. Going on — proceeding in a certain way.

A wave, an ocean breaker of lavender. And the heat in the valley. Stunning. Stunted. The heat like a blow to the head.

You hear yourself for the first time.

What have you failed to get hold of? The sudden rush of time. Its out-of-control-ness. You find yourself run up the shore, high up. Have you described your position adequately enough?

Already your flesh tastes of salt because the wind is rising off the sea. The sea appearing on the right suddenly. Washing the edge of the plain. Twin lagoons and a town built between them. The old walls of the public gardens, ornamented, rusticated. And the far end of the town, like a stern jutting into the lagoon. Walled, with fraying palms, graffiti, litter.

But with the sun going down and the light mistily blue on the lagoon the scruffy town becomes Venice or Stockholm. Venice in poverty. A destitute Stockholm.

The paper-dryness of your shirt.

Everything in relation to the idea that we must make something of ourselves in the time we have — we must civilise ourselves, we must raise ourselves up.

The corniche running up from the lagoons, climbing up beside an almost-beach of grey pumice. Grand shuttered houses on the peninsular, orange, yellow — shuttered and planted about with palms and cypresses.

And then falling into the deep-water port with a madonna at the end of the harbour wall facing out to sea. The fishing fleet, the sense of identity of the port bound up in the row of trawlers. Work. The positioning of yourself, the placing of things. Being in relation to everything else.

The civic hall and new promenade and more palms and the modern church because the old one was razed by war.

And the boats return, draw into the harbour and turn into their moorings. White boats streaked with rust, upturned white prows on blue water. And two boats turn together, slowly - a trawlerman's ballet — long practiced — and moor slowly at the quay wall.

And you're struck by the simple, straightforward placing of one thing in relation to another.

You see the value in the way things are simply placed. You see you must place yourself clearly and resolutely in relation to everything else. You see that this placing of yourself in the world is your only reasonable concern. All other concerns live inside this concern.

*The city in the lagoon is ringed around by crumbling balustrades.
At the head of the causeway there stands a red house with burnt
dark red walls, a sluice house or pump house or toll collector,
completely alone facing out over the dark shallow water of the
south lagoon with the heaped boxes and buttressed towers of the
lagoon city all piled up behind it.*

EXPERIMENTAL WRITING

FEAR HAS LEFT YOU

The characteristic set of your mouth before speaking.

Rain outside.

*You say, In A Very Real Sense, There Are Only The
Circumstances Of Your Feeling.*

*You say, Some Feeling Exists With So Much Force, Reality Is
Shaped By It.*

The built landscapes of cities.

Books, cinemas.

*You say, We Have Lost Our Dedication To One Thing. In Place
of a Single Cause, a Wealth of Causes.*

Our lives spent in the intensification of life.

*Sometimes you marvel at the distance it's possible to cover in
talk alone.*

*You say, We Must Have The Courage Not To Fail In
The Moment.*

*You say, We Have No Time For Anything Other Than
This Reasonableness.*

This City.

Outside, the sound of sanity falling again. Reasonableness tumbling out of the sky.

The sky blazes in one direction only. The river is full of light.

You say It Is As If Fear Has Left You.

You say, It Is As If There Could Be No Parting, No Lasting End, Only The Endless Sailing Out Of Feeling.

DARE

What would you and what wouldn't you dare to do? Go to Paris. Lecture in English in Paris, walk by the Seine. Make friends. Enemies.

PARIS

Eventually they go to Paris. Eventually they do go there.

In the cold. Sky bleached with cold. In the rain. In a cafe where the coffee is good but expensive.

It is immensely, devastatingly cold. We walk out anyway.

They walk out into the rain.

I wished for there to be rain, for Paris to be as awful as possible. I wanted Paris to be cruel, unforgiving.

We walk in the rain towards the river.

They walk towards the river in a high wind.

The water is whipped up between its banks. The banks are very close together, astonishingly close. There are so many bridges.

A woman squats in the gutter and urinates. The stained backs of houses buttress the Île de la Cité. The wind comes in squalls. The rain is heavier now.

Paris is nothing. A cold northern European city.

They call out over the Seine. Call out. Say, Rise Paris. The rain comes down harder. But Paris has stirred herself.

Wars, revolutions, crimes, famines, corruptions, colonialism, exploitation, books, pictures, cafes. Paris stirs herself.

Artist's models, writers, theorists, infidelities, poor food, overpriced rooms with no heat, little reviews, manifestos, Gertrude Stein.

The fictional city of Paris, expensive, foreign, cold, damp, the impossible city of Paris, rises.

Paris is just a city.

They see Paris for the first time. The city. The grey river divided by its islands and strangled by the proximity of its banks.

They see Paris for the first time. As it rains and the wind blows and the divided river flows on.

one one one one one one one one one one one one one one one one
one one one one one one one one one one one one one one one one
one one one one one one one one one one one one one one one one
one one one one one one one one one one one one one one one one
one one one one one one one one one one one one one one one one
one one one one one one one one one one one one one one one one
one one one one one one one one one one one one one one one one
one one one one one one one one one one one one one one one one
one one one one one one one one one one one one one one one one
one one one one one one one one one one one one one one one one
one one one one one one one one one one one one one one one one
one one one one one one one one one one one one one one one one
one one one one one one one one one one one one one one one one

/paris

*one one one one one one one one one one one one one one one one
one one one one one one one one one one one one one one one one
one one one one one one one one one one one one one one one one
one one one one one one one one one one one one one one one one
one one one one one one one one one one one one one one one one
one one one one one one one one one one one one one one one one
one one one one one one one one one one one one one one one one
one one one one one one one one one one one one one one one one
one one one one one one one one one one one one one one one one
one one one one one one one one one one one one one one one one
one one one one one one one one one one one one one one one one
one one one one one one one one one one one one one one one one*

*[Editor's note: these repetitions of the word 'one' appear at the end of the
original manuscript of 'Paris'. Their purpose is unclear – and now forgotten by
the author – but the decision was taken to retain them here in order to present
the essay as written twenty years ago.]*

OR
(What is the alternative?)

Or you see a comet blaze up and die in the black sky. And the frost hard on the verges at the roadside.

Or you find a swallow dead on a cloud of ash in the metal box of the stove. And struggle against the immensity of the cold, when the house is cold into its foundations.

Or you sit watching the sea between shaking rhododendron bushes, grey like the sky, dragging by the headland with waves turning and breaking evenly all over it.

Or you see (with hindsight) that it is all only possible with hindsight — perhaps the whole world exists only in hindsight.

Or you think about not wanting to become thickened, slowed by time, a mind capable of more but missing the lightness, the ability to flutter around things.

Or you see the dog-earedness of the buildings, and the small native oysters, and the fantastically expensive champagne because Champagne is four thousand miles away. And you are on the edge of the world, ludicrously high up.

Or you see that everything anyone ever says is always self-referential.

Or you're taken to lunch at a theatre club behind an unmarked door somewhere near Seven Dials.

Or you buy tea called Russian Caravan.

Or you eat lunch in the square at Sienna, gazing up at a single light showing high up behind a half shuttered balcony and you wonder about the life under the naked light bulb.

Or you read menus in French, asparagus soup, beef wellington, crêpes suzette.

Or you walk the length of corridors overhung with vaulting like giant ribs, ribbed like the inside of a whale.

Or you stand outside the British Museum.

Or you read Collette in the afternoon, drinking.

Or you watch the sun lower itself into the sea rolling like oil, and the mist is up by the headland in spite of summer, in spite of this being only a little later than the longest day.

Or you lie still, tormented by a knock at the door. Or a chance meeting in the street. Or you drink in the afternoon. You make margaritas with limes like green outsized hens' eggs.

Or you gaze up at the drawn blinds with the sun blazing behind and the wind blowing in the trees, and the room hot and dark with the droning of the fan, the one that leaks oil.

Or you summon all your courage to step out into the world.

Or you remember, you remind yourself, you once said to yourself, you wanted only to know how to live.

Or you cannot continue at all.

Or you eat again in the little cafe above the green. And buy fish. And drive for a short while (and drive well).

Or you buy white lilac, a wisteria.

Or you see that everything is one thing.

Or you tear up to the Rainbow Room with your ears ringing. To be a tourist.

Or you remark that the stained ramparts remind you of black and white pictures in a book about Paris.

Or you look out over the bridges way below, the prow of Manhattan, the twin towers of the World Trade Center. And the cloud running in. And the most beautiful thing of all is the cloud running in.

A COLETTE AFTERNOON

'*If it wasn't a deadly prize, wouldn't that beautiful young
boy plead for a cup with poisoned water to spend one night
with Cleopatra?*'

*The wind is very fierce in the trees outside. The blinds drawn
upward, angled against the sun.*

Rancid almond in a croissant, masked by good coffee.

And the trees thrashing, flailing in the heat.

Duty, suppositions, inequalities –

*Wouldn't that beautiful boy – the golden barge, galley slaves, silks,
anointing the emblematic little crease at the top of the arm where
the flesh of the arm joins the flesh of the torso –*

*The smell of chocolate and lilies. The clock caught forever
at 3.16.*

*The attempt to cover up time. Not so bad really, not in
flat light. Square on. If I face you squarely and the light is
flat enough –*

Wouldn't that beautiful boy plead for the cup with water –

Another glass of wine.

No time. No point in the future.

The sun thrown up onto the ceiling. Can't take the exhaustion, but can't take the settlement either — the settling of the world, the falling back of the world onto its haunches.

Then suddenly something occurs between the light and the heat outside and the great beauty of the room — the chinoiserie lamp, made from a rescued biscuit tin, the cushion cut from a nineteenth-century Turkish smoking jacket —

Something —

There ought to have been halva, Turkish delight scented with rose, cherries, intensely sweet dates, a stream of well-wishers — to pay homage —

To the courage of the beautiful boy as he pleads for the marked cup —

The marked cup —

The marked cup —

Pleading for the —

Take O take those lips away — those eyes —

Dates and French bread, coffee and Pineau de Charentes in a little Victorian glass. The dates are very sweet, intensely, stickily sweet.

Take O take —

*The Pineau is strange in its roughness/bitterness, sweetwayness;
the sweet laying over the first crude fermentation, the raw heat of
it. Acetone.*

He had always loved her. He would love her unto death —

*Lunch at an extraordinary hour (lunch in the afternoon) the work
put away and done with, lunch at the perennial hour of 3.16.
Curious choices for lunch: dates and stale bread. Complete
government of the hour.*

*The cup with poison, taken the life to fracture. Fractured but still
whole. As if the vision were disturbed. Migraine. A fissure in the
earth. As true as the cup is marked.*

*And wouldn't he willingly beg for the cup with poisoned water to
spend one night with Cleopatra anyway?*

The huge capacity — rapaciousness — to feel.

It is 3.16.

The nothing-holding, the immediacy, sudden nowness.

*He asked God to help him and God said, I sent you Cleopatra,
what more do you want?*

A broken decanter, empty cups, paper, letters – sealed in vain –

La belle époque. Always 3.16. Always la belle époque –

There, stepping out of life.

In another world of immediacy, sudden appearance, bitter, devastating absences.

Everything returns to absence. Anything is more significant by its absence, by what is not said and what is not accomplished.

A Colette Afternoon – Paris bitter outside. Everything shuttered against the rain. Fires that smoke or burn lazily, make more draught than warmth.

Living on bread and hope.

We'll call the room Corsica and be happy in the work, and on the French Island we'll drink sparkling wine and cognac, eat the dates from the little silver dish. Good strong coffee and a high bright day. Blue sky and a high bright day. Blue sky in the morning and huge thunderous clouds. The wind bright in the chaotic trees, even the cypress moves, detaching a branch to sway out from the whole, returning darkly.

Toast, hot and buttered, spread with anchovy. Gentlemen's relish. A bowl of black grapes. Some whipped cream.

Spinach, king of vegetables.

What is it about Colette?

A Colette Afternoon – absurd, childish. Something to do with possession, self-possession in the face of everything. Will. Unbending in the face of the world –

BILLETS-DOUX

1.

The Flore, or the Deux Magots, or Florian in Venice with its small rooms painted after the four seasons, or the little green-painted salon at the Cafe de l'Opera opposite the opera house in Barcelona, or any of those little cafes, unremarkable really, except for what they mean about the continual renewal of talking.

2.

Lunch on the terrace above the beach at Barcelona; oysters at the Cafe de la Paix by the opera in Paris; long heated-up afternoons above the sea at Capri, walking from the Via Tragara to the Villa Krupp (was it Gorky's villa?), walking in airless contemplation of what next, hope, more than a little love and the sea, as if bluer than God intended, blown out from the island a thousand feet below.

3.

French Hanoi. Pictures of French Hanoi, the French Colonies. You say you have always to be close to one of the great centres like London or Paris. Colonialism, sticky with exoticism still: Saigon was the Paris of the Far East. A thousand years of Paris, two thousand years of London.

4.

Oysters – natives – the grey-beige flesh curled neatly in the half shells. The huge painted salon – green and gilt. Bitterly cold champagne. The sea-taste of the oysters. And your good fortune, the obligation to let no detail of it pass unremarked. The truth of cities. You say you want to live on an answering scale. You say you want to understand, to have strength, on the vast scale of cities.

5.

Barcelona, Paris, Berlin, Rome, London. You say, we have no time for anything other than this reasonableness: our built lives, our manufactured, assembled lives. The heroic vastness and truth of cities. The hotel built by the river in a kind of opulent, emphatic bad taste. The zoo strung with green neon, once the largest zoo in the world.

6.

Flying in low over the Arid Plains. A broken path to an unmarked door. The incongruous cafe-sound of spoken French. Jazz on the car radio. Fretted minarets. Decaying European boulevards — apartment buildings like the big Haussmann blocks in Paris decaying slowly in the heat. And a strange, raffish, colonial feeling about the journey, brought on by the jazz. French banking and language, English law. You say for you North Africa is the paleness of the egrets at dusk, in the egret tree, by the roadside, beyond the green neon advertising the splendours of Giza zoo.

LAS PALMAS

We might have left Paris and travelled here by train a hundred years ago. Arriving with the freight, mineral, and coal wagons. Menus in French from the 1860s. A great deal of asparagus soup. Picture windows facing the blowing palms and a flattish, greyish sea.

The ghost of la belle époque (indecently plump chairs) laid over the frugal ghosts of the Dominicans (cloisters with all the detail in the stonework rubbed away by time; huge, meaningless, heroic amounts of time). We could have taken holy orders if it weren't for the endless round of cocktails, bottles and bottles of spumante, cigars, the gloriously bad pianist playing in the cloister.

And all the time working. Knowing there's no way out except right through the other side of it. The stinging effort and the vaguely-felt hopelessness of it.

Gales high up above the bay. Very beautiful gardens of torn hibiscus and wrecked date palms. Only the heart of the palm grows; if the palm loses its heart, it loses everything.

Last night there were fireworks burning near the sea. Great chrysanthemums of fire. The red light travelled to us most easily through the hot, thin atmosphere. Supper on a tiny terrace above the roof tops, a smart little restaurant, 'founded in 1953' with terrific pride. Carpaccio of fish, a lobster ravioli with splinters of pungent black truffle, a treacly dessert wine called very beautifully Duca di Castelmonte.

The coastline reminds me (or perhaps I like the idea that it reminds me) of the thickly sounding 'Cabeza de Lobo' in Tennessee Williams' Suddenly Last Summer. The public and private beaches. Paying for beds and cubicles. The locals, very dark, with hair sculpted into curious ridges and sinister little devils horns. The black and white postcards — turn-of-the-century reproductions — of stark naked youths, alone or in groups, standing or reclining on chunks of rock, some with pan-pipes and jutting bellies. And always above everything, the mountain blowing smoke rings, flying streamers over her head, the wind gusting down from her flanks, shaking the gardens up.

However much we drink we don't become blissfully oblivious or abandoned to our fate. We drink and we become exhausted but we don't become drunk. We have become completely incapable of drunkenness. We are irrevocably sober. Terrifyingly, irremediably sober.

Of course it's all been said before. Of course it all makes not a scrap of difference. But what else is there?

From the Teatro Greco you can see the entire coastline, and between the Ionian columns... the Ionian Sea. Even Plato came to Sicily. Platonic Sicily. Uneasy, fleshy, platonic Sicily. I wake up in *my room in the early hours trying to be clear about the difficulties – head full of spumante – startled awake by the attempt to be clear. The impossibility of saying or meaning anything clearly to anyone. Pay heed in some way (still unclear) to apparent, or real absences, significant intervals. Something that knows itself, is the knowing of itself, is most intensely itself.*

And then you run up against the impossibility of trying to hold onto anything you might discover. Wanting to hold and fix an idea with the 'right' words even though the right words don't exist or are too encumbered. There's a world of difference between regarding words with a kind of blind, hapless faith, and using them (because there's no other way of going on), aware of the difficulties, shortfalls, traps.

It is impossible to sit on the beach looking out over the 'Isola Bella' (and it is very beautiful) without being forever reminded of the trains running over the strip of pebbly flat below. The pebbles blotched or swamped with oil before the land rises suddenly. Freight trains always make me think of Mussolini's Italy, half-heartedly industrialised, hoping for global dominance, but somehow not entirely willing to do what it is necessary to do for global dominance. And perhaps I am not so different from Mussolini's Italy myself, hoping for great things for (and from) myself but not entirely willing to do what it is necessary to do.

We walk up to the Greek amphitheatre in incredible heart, half dazed. An expedition along Forsterian lines (Charlotte Bartlett and Lucy Honeychurch open themselves to physical sensation at the Teatro Greco: they are overwrought by the heat and the louche postcards in every shop window).

Imagine the little outing accompanied by the ludicrous easy-listening strains of Shostakovich's *Jazz Suit*. Alice Toklas in her ominously named 'Spanish Disguise' (enormous lobe-bearing gypsy earrings, artificial flowers in her hat). And Gertrude Stein, mistaken (gloriously and not entirely unreasonably) for some kind of religious leader. And in the heat and surrounded by the broken stones, fox-trotting to the Shostakovich (very slowly and decorously) everyone leading, nobody following.

In Italy for the first time – stifling in an Italian train – Alice B. Toklas (the 'B' is for Babette) abandoned her corset to the retreating countryside. The train sailing by and Alice B's corset tumbling heroically over the vines and olives. An end to imposed restraint and rigidity. An end to the old structures. Everything to be made new. Gertrude Stein said, I am violently devoted to the new. The worst of convention, like Alice's cherry red corset, collapsed in the dust.

If you experiment in any way, you are always working into an undefined space. You can try to say where the edges might be but *you can't stand firm on anything other than truth, however implausible or difficult to grasp.*

Reasonableness is no guarantee of truth.

When the rain comes unexpectedly it stings our backs. It rains for hours. Everything drenched. Beaten down. Done-for. Overflowing pipe work and ruined stucco. Beautifully ruined. In London it would be plain rot: blistering stucco flowered with moss, somewhere in Bloomsbury on a dank Wednesday afternoon. Here it's raffish, swaggering decay. Leaves helter-skelter out of the trees. Cloister cocktail bar and poorly old piano swimming, veneers peeling. Gravel jumping, rainwater pouring into the grill at the base of the well as if the whole world were being drawn down – loose change, mislaid keys, breadcrumbs, pride, skill, failure, disappointment, self-importance.

Is the force you speak with more important than the thing you say? Is that the answer? Do you have enough courage for that to be it?

It follows any answer is an answer. Any answer is an answer, is an answer.

When you are raw, unformed, you expect or want things to be smooth, perfect, invincible. Then, as you discover what's really important, you come to care about the human in things. You care more for the confused, ugly struggle for understanding. You come to appreciate intensity – something's being most completely what it is – more than beauty. Effort isn't smooth, knowing, efficient, but wasteful, difficult, feckless, complacent, desperate, idle, half-hearted, committed, vague.

Waves turning unseen in the dark against the shale beaches. Another glass of Italian brandy, another espresso. Hot air blowing up from the sea. Sauntering devils. A cross on the hill.

What does it mean? What does any of it mean? Less and less… is an answer. Everything returns to absence is an answer.

Debussy described music as the spaces between the notes. Marguerite Duras said the only solution to the problem of writing is to say nothing, except that can't be written down.

Mightn't the arrangements understanding chooses for itself be better than the ones we would otherwise choose for it? Something that helps the understanding needn't necessarily have meaning attached to it. What helps the understanding may even be necessarily obscure. It's perfectly possible to understand something profoundly in the absence of meaning, and equally possible to mean or attempt to signify something in the complete absence of understanding.

I had wanted to make a language so finely wrought, so immaculate in its lyricism that it would catch the outline of everything like a covering of finely woven silk. I had hoped some kind of understanding would show itself in sharp relief. When it didn't, I put myself in the safe hands of Gertrude Stein and I tried to make a new language. But the new language was always flawed – different flaws but flaws just the same. Perhaps the first step of all is to allow language to stand for itself: chant, articulation, tone. Only this. Face value.

Perhaps it's necessary to battle against the accumulation of meaning even though you must inevitably lose the battle. A kind of chipping away at the accumulation of meaning until exhausted, you give up all hope in the language, in the hope of something greater, something with greater spaces in it, disencumbered, an expanded sense, a free, open steppe into which anything however problematic or unwieldy might fit.

The moon rose slowly, big and slung low in the sky. One of those short, hot summer nights that never gets properly dark.

When I opened the door to the little stove there was a swallow trapped inside, caught as if in mid-flight, wings outstretched, frozen like a photograph. And so unsalvageably sad – summer caught up in the mechanics of stove pipe and stove, laid out over the soft ruins of the burnt-out anthracite.

She said there'd be such wonderful things to find on the beach after the summer storms. And I saw them – charms, rarities –leaping *up from the shingle into her arms.*

It is a battle for independence, all of it, everything comes back to the battle for our own territory. The rules whatever they are don't apply here. The rules, whatever they are, are to be remade. We're out on our own.

Perhaps it is only possible to deal in fragments, in the intervals or spaces between things. And it's the strung-out-ness of fragments, the fracturedness of them, rather than the substance of the fragments themselves that makes something possible. Between fragments, all possible sense lies. Between fragments, nothing is prescribed, completed, done with. Everything is half-seen, open.

I found a little watercolour called 'Las Palmas'. Ominous violet (violent) storm clouds out to sea with the sun behind. The light spreading out in pillars and in the distance, at the horizon, the sea flat in the eye of the storm with the light full on it. The town stands mounded up in the foreground, minarets, rakish palms, Morocco, North Africa. Moorish, Spanish. Las palmas standing up stiffly against the sky. Stiffish, happy palms blowing in the hot wind. Grasshoppers big as locusts, moths like small birds, the storm threatening just offshore, then the palm leaves will be torn, screaming reedily from the trees. The little picture dated 1908. The difficulties of the journey to Las Palmas in 1908. The trains, connections, boat-trains, Pullmans, sleepers, steamers, porters, trunks, mules and the attendant, pioneering courage. O no, not me! And the chap who sold me Las Palmas — a great conversational swimmer, splashing about with the enthusiasm and inquisitiveness of a child. Everything new, to be discovered and understood. The wonder of 1908 and summer, this summer.

It's not what a thing is but the intensity with which it is. Absence, interval, fracture and silence — the substance of these things doesn't matter, only the intensity with which they are what they are. The deliberate making of space so that something very great can flow in. Not a new language but the deliberate making or reallocating of space inside language.

For the first time I regretted the passing of another summer. Perhaps because this had seemed a year of losses. I wanted there to be some kind of compensation. Great, unbroken stretches of affection and loyalty. I wanted there to be heroism. A great era of heroism, courage, friendship, epic resilience, originality.

UNSAID

The mill stood on the first bank of higher land behind the sea. With its main sails still. And the little spread of its fan tail. Like the tail of an ornamental dove fanned out for courtship. The agent showed us the millhouse built to the side and then the tower rooms, the higher the smaller, reached by ladders and loose cords of rope as thick as a man's arm.

Each room had a greasy hand basin and an electric bar fire. A high, diminished, dizzying boarding house of turned rooms.

The agent said he would show us the cap, the wooden, upkeeled-boat roof which used to turn as the sails followed the wind. And once we had peered at its wooden ribs under felt and the locked wheels on circular rails, we stepped out onto the platform.

The fan tail loomed above us, larger and heavier than it appeared from the ground. Hard thick timbers holding the paddles of the fan. Weight above. White. Light-filled. The sun burning between the angles of the blades. Heavy. Huge. Robust. And so very little underfoot. A thin board. We were higher than the woods. Wind. Fierce sun. The land risen and falling to the blue hearth-tile of the sea. The train whistling, full of steam and trippers. The lane nothing but sand, running down and away to the sea. Most of all the sea. The sunny circular room underfoot with its ringed basin and bar fire.

I became certain that my intention to write was an honest and a good one — a perfectly valuable intention that had its existence somehow elsewhere. Inside. Weighty. Unreachable. Inarticulable. The depth of what ought to be given. A greater complexity and weight of intuition that defies the word itself.

Then we had to come away, let ourselves down the ladders by the heavy, dropping lines of rope, walking briefly in the garden burned dry by the summer. And away, knowing we would never live there, never work in the tower rooms, never make our lives there.

Knowing something is unsaid is not the same as nothing being said. The knowing makes the something unsaid discernible; meaningfully silent not just silent, like the empty bottles that give away the alcoholic.

MARTIN FIRRELL

Martin Firrell (born 4 April 1963, Paris, France) has been described variously as a cultural activist, a campaigner, a public artist, or benevolent provocateur, stimulating debate in public space to promote positive social change.

Firrell has raised questions about the politics of ageing, individual liberty, the right to personal idiosyncrasy, cultural diversity, gender and LGBT+ equality, faith, climate change, masculinity, the rights of women, what constitutes a meaningful and purposeful life, hero worship, fair and truthful government, and the quality of human lived experience.

He has been described by The Guardian Newspaper, London, as 'One of the capital's most influential public artists'.

His mature work has been summarised as 'art as debate'.
www.martinfirrell.com

www.ingramcontent.com/pod-product-compliance
Lightning Source LLC
Chambersburg PA
CBHW031354060726

47590CB00007B/2770